Masquerade Masks

An Adult Coloring Book Featuring Fun and Relaxing Masquerade and Mardi Gras Mask Designs

MantraCraft®

MantraCraft®

This Coloring Book belongs to:

_____

_____

_____

_____

SOME HELPFUL TIPS

Use a backing sheet behind the image that you are coloring on. This will help protect other images if colors happen to bleed through, especially if you are using wet colors, markers, or alcohol based colors.

In case you'd like to remove the image from the book before coloring, you can use an X-ACTO/similar knife to make a clean cut close to the spine. You can then place this removed image on a clipboard and use backing sheets to provide firm support and easy coloring.

You can use a variety of color types with this coloring book. While we recommend colored pencils for best results, you can also use other color types like gel pens, markers. Just make sure you use a thick backing sheet to prevent bleed through.

Before you start, use the color test page on the opposite page to get a fair idea of how your colors will appear on the images within. You can also use the color test page to build your swatch and record the various color combinations that you use for this coloring book.

Happy Coloring!

MantraCraft® Team

Color Test Page

MARDI
GRAS

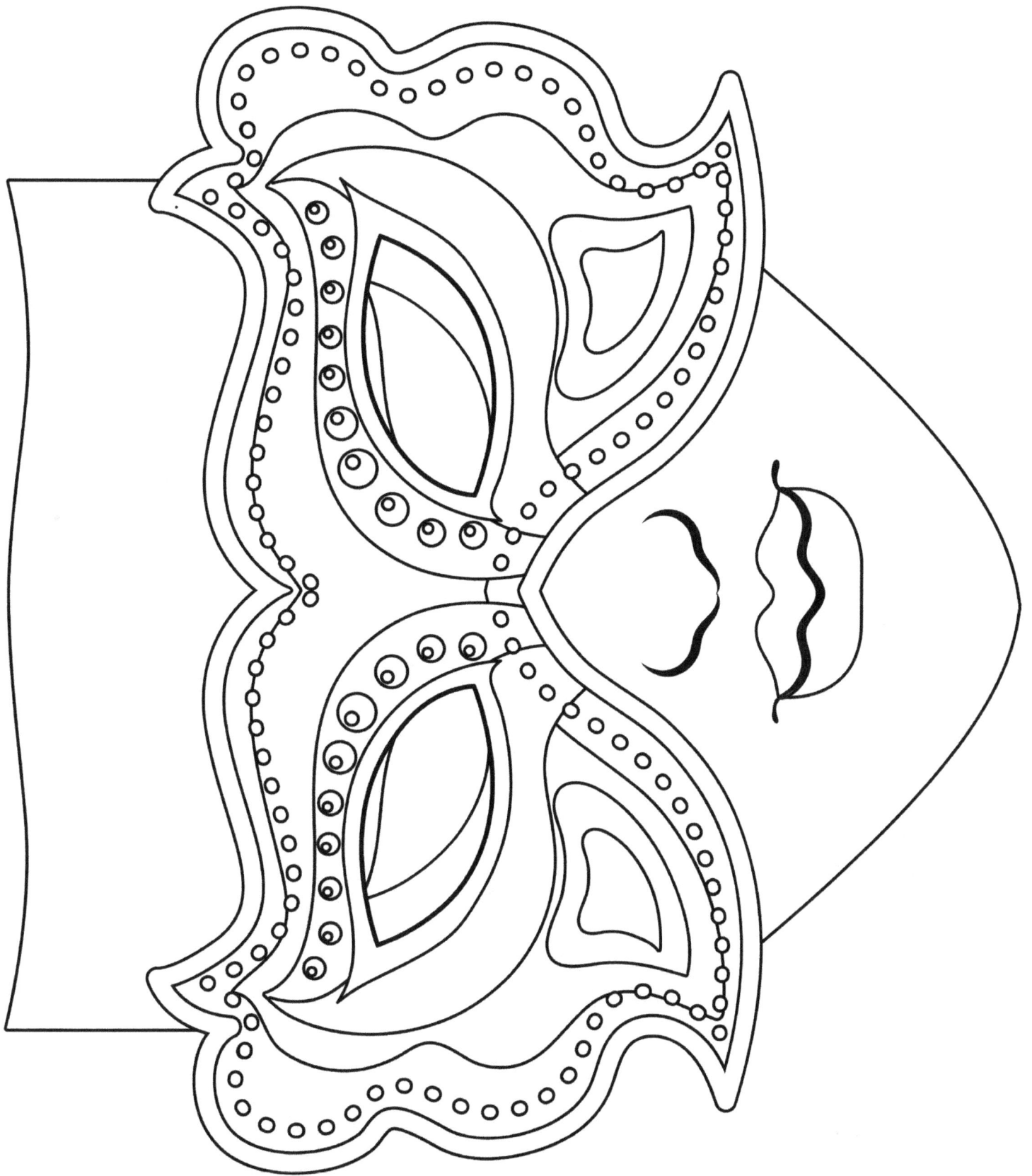

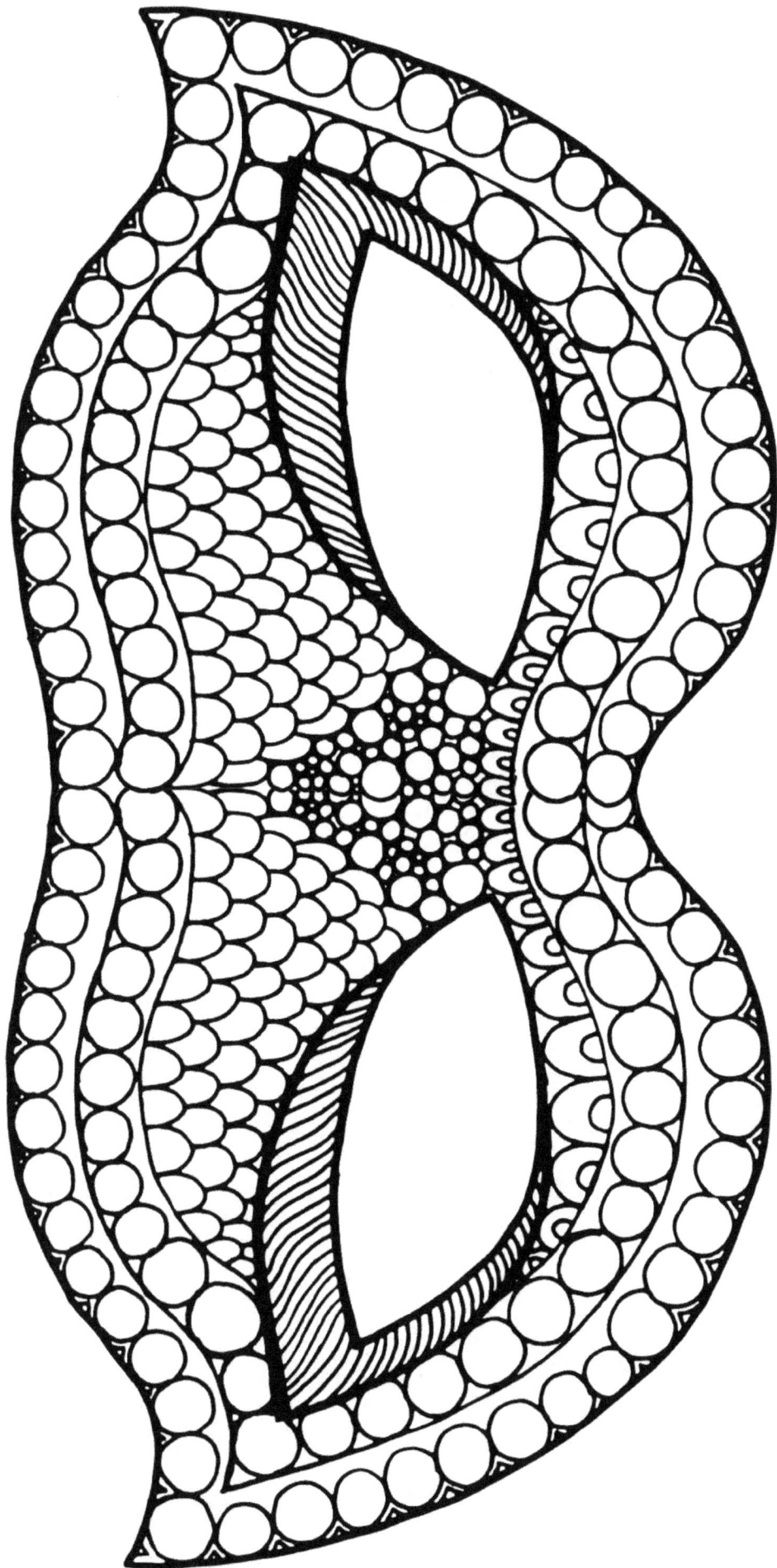

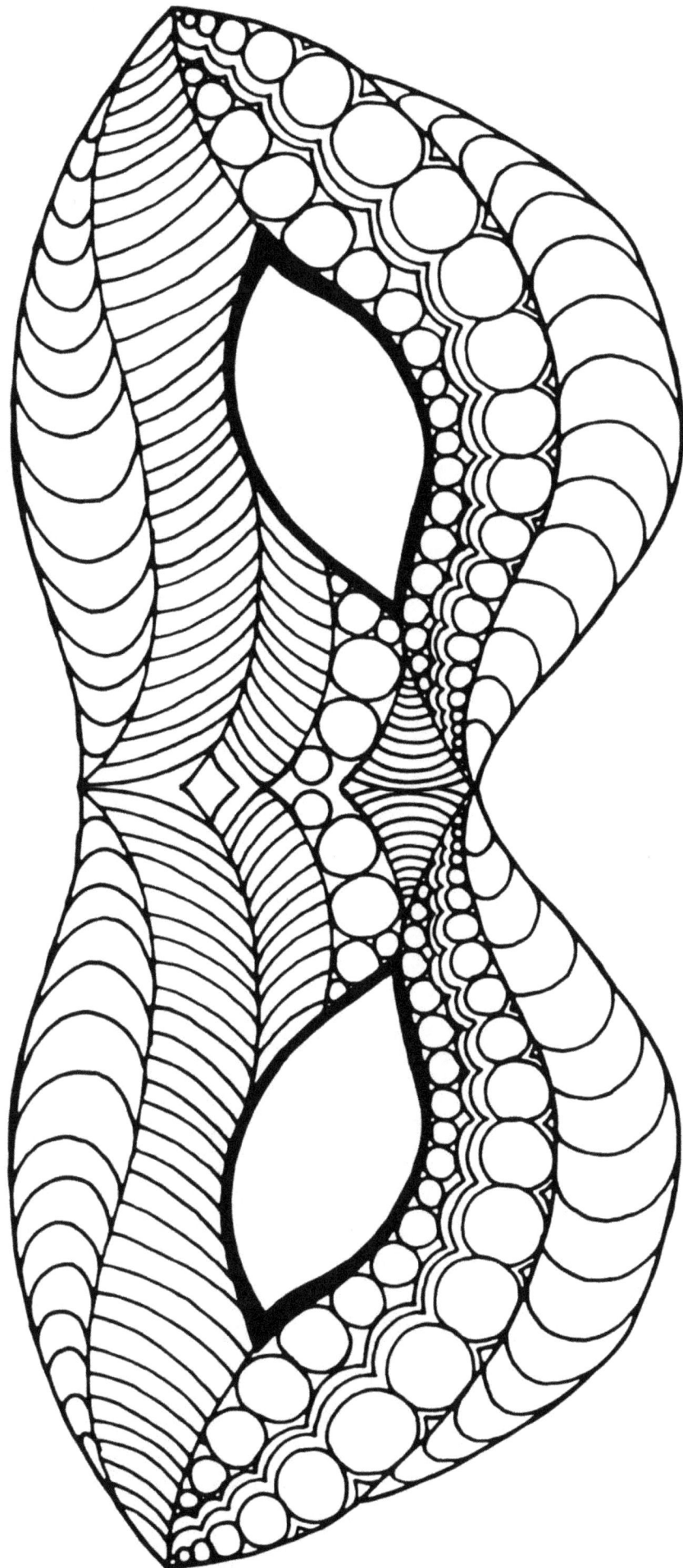

REVIEW THIS COLORING BOOK

Your reviews matter. Please take a moment to review this book. It's simple. Just visit the website where you purchased it from, find the book listing, and submit a review. This not only helps MantraCraft® continue to create amazing books for you, but also helps other colorists discover us.

Thanks for your support, and for sharing your thoughts!

JOIN MANTRACRAFT GROUP

Join MantraCraft® Coloring Books Facebook community to connect with coloring book enthusiasts, showcase your masterpieces, share coloring tips, and discover your next coloring adventure.

You can find us on: **Facebook.com/groups/MantraCraft**

Or simply search for MantraCraft Coloring Books Group on Facebook.

JOIN MANTRACRAFT EMAIL LIST

Join MantraCraft® email list by visiting **MantraCraft.com**

Joining our email list is the best way to stay informed about latest releases and promotions.

MantraCraft®

About MantraCraft®

MantraCraft® creates a wide range of beautiful coloring books that help you relax, unwind, and express your creativity. MantraCraft® coloring books are loved by coloring book enthusiasts and they are frequent best-sellers.

Visit our website **mantracraft.com** to explore the entire MantraCraft Coloring Books catalog, and sign up for our email list.

Join MantraCraft® Coloring Books community to connect with coloring book enthusiasts, showcase your masterpieces, share coloring tips, and discover your next coloring adventure.

Facebook.com/groups/MantraCraft

Facebook.com/MantraCraftColoringBooks

@MantraCraft